Original title:
Shifting Serenity



Author: Elias Marchant

ISBN HARDBACK: 978-9916-90-724-5
ISBN PAPERBACK: 978-9916-90-725-2

## Harmonies from the Heart

In quiet whispers, dreams take flight,
Melodies dance in the soft moonlight.
Strings of laughter, a gentle sway,
Echoes of love in the night play.

Voices blend in a tender grace,
Binding souls in a warm embrace.
Each note a story, subtly told,
Harmonies deep, like treasures of gold.

## Thought Bubbles of Soft Transition

Like wisps of clouds in a gentle breeze,
Thoughts drift softly, aiming to please.
Transforming moments, fleeting and bright,
Casting shadows in the fading light.

With pastel dreams and colors that blend,
Nature’s palette, where time can bend.
Floating away on a sigh and a thought,
In this silence, magic is caught.

## A Haiku in Motion

Whispers of the trees,
Carried on the winds of change,
Nature's heart beats free.

Petals fall like thoughts,
Scattering in soft sunlight,
Time’s gentle embrace.

## The Lanterns of a Soft Night

Stars flicker like lanterns, bright and clear,
Guiding lost souls, drawing them near.
In the hush of the evening's sigh,
Dreams awaken beneath the sky.

The moon, a guardian, watches close,
Casting shadows, a gentle dose.
Each glow a promise, softly shared,
In the night's embrace, we are bared.

## Harmony in Flux

In the dance of shifting winds,
Nature sings her lullabies.
Colors blend where light begins,
Embracing change as daylight dies.

Ripples flow through verdant fields,
Whispers of the earth resound.
Each season yields what time unveils,
A symphony of life unbound.

Stars above in night’s embrace,
Watch the world transform anew.
In every heartbeat, every trace,
Harmony in flux shines through.

## The Quiet Unraveling

Threads of silence softly fray,
In corners where the shadows creep.
Moments slip like grains of clay,
Time, a secret we must keep.

Whispers tell of dreams undone,
Colors fade with gentle grace.
The moon retreats, the night is spun,
A quiet unraveling takes place.

In the stillness, truths emerge,
Like petals falling to the ground.
From chaos, a new life will surge,
In the quiet, we are found.

## Echoes of Gentle Change

Softly echoes across the glade,
Nature stirs with tender sighs.
In whispers, old and new invade,
Life’s sweet cadence never dies.

Leaves cascade in golden light,
Each one speaks of time’s embrace.
In twilight’s glow, day turns to night,
A gentle change we all must face.

Moments linger in the breeze,
Carrying tales from far away.
In this dance, our hearts find ease,
Echoes of change come out to play.

## Murmurs of a Restless Breeze

In the hush of twilight's grace,
A restless breeze begins to roam.
It whispers secrets in this place,
Of distant lands and dreams of home.

Through the trees, its voice resounds,
A melody both soft and clear.
Stirring leaves on hallowed grounds,
It carries laughter, joy, and fear.

Waves of change in every sigh,
Awakening the slumbering hearts.
In the murmur, we learn to fly,
As the restless breeze departs.

## Winds of Change

In the whisper of the trees,
A promise dances with the breeze.
Old paths crumble, new ones rise,
As time unveils its vast disguise.

Seasons shift and colors blend,
Courage found, as shadows end.
Life's embrace, both fierce and kind,
In every step, the light we find.

Dreams ascend on wings of hope,
Through starlit skies, we learn to cope.
Change, a friend, though clad in fear,
Awaits us all, forever near.

With every sigh, a chance to see,
A world reborn, wild and free.
Embrace the winds, let them arrange,
The beauty found in winds of change.

## Beneath the Surface

Silent depths, where shadows play,
A hidden world, where secrets lay.
Ripples tell of tales untold,
A universe, both dark and bold.

Whispers soft in currents move,
Mysteries, they seek to prove.
Beneath the calm, a storm resides,
In silent depths, the truth abides.

Coral dreams and fish that dart,
Life swirls deep within our heart.
Glimmers flash, both bright and rare,
Awakening our primal care.

Dive within, where few will go,
Find the treasures buried slow.
For in these depths, we might just learn,
The lessons life so dearly yearns.

## Fleeting Calm

In the hush of evening's glow,
Quiet moments gently flow.
Stars ignite the velvet night,
Cocooned in peace, the heart takes flight.

Time stands still, like rippling streams,
Cradled softly in our dreams.
Thoughts, like fireflies, drift and sway,
In this pause, we find our way.

Breathe in deep, the fragrant air,
Let go of worries, shed your care.
In fleeting calm, we craft our fate,
As silence weaves threads of heart's state.

But dawn awaits; shadows grow long,
Yet in this peace, we find our song.
Hold it close, this transient balm,
For life's true beauty lies in calm.

## Tides of Reflection

Waves that rise, then slip away,
Mirror thoughts of yesterday.
What's been lost, what remains whole,
Tides of time shape every soul.

Footprints washed upon the shore,
Echoes of what was before.
With every swell, a memory,
Casting visions, wild and free.

In moonlit glow, we find our place,
Tracing truth on water's face.
Each splash a story, every wave,
Bringing forth what we must save.

As oceans churn, with ebb and flow,
Reflections whisper what we know.
Ride the tides, where thoughts converge,
In their depth, our dreams emerge.

## The Breath of Twilight

The sun dips low in silent grace,
Whispers of dusk begin to trace.
Shadows stretch, the day will fade,
In twilight's soft and gentle shade.

Stars awake, they twinkle bright,
Piercing through the cloak of night.
A hush falls deep across the land,
As dreams and night begin to stand.

## Floating on Serene Waters

Gentle ripples kiss the shore,
Nature sings, a soft encore.
Beneath the sky, the calm reflects,
In stillness, every heart connects.

A swan glides by, so pure and free,
In harmony with the melody.
The world dissolves in liquid light,
As day surrenders to the night.

## Dance of the Unseen

A breeze stirs whispers in the trees,
The hidden dance, a quiet tease.
Moonlight casts its silvery spell,
In secret realms, the spirits dwell.

Cloaked in shadows, magic thrives,
In every heartbeat, wonder lives.
With every step, the unseen sways,
In beauty's grasp, their dance conveys.

## Embracing Variance

Colors swirl in life's great art,
Harmony found in every part.
Chaos and peace, a vibrant quilt,
In contrasts, the heart is built.

Seasons change with rhythms pure,
In every twist, we find the cure.
Embracing all that life imparts,
In every note, the music starts.

## Lullabies of the Mind

In shadows soft, thoughts gently play,
Whispers of dreams drift and sway.
Hushed melodies weave through the night,
Cradling souls till morning light.

Silent secrets in moonlit skies,
Guarded wishes in sweet lullabies.
Rest now, heart, in tranquil repose,
As peace unfolds and softly flows.

## The Whispering Change

Leaves murmur tales of seasons passed,
Time's gentle fingers hold fast.
Breezes soften the edge of day,
Carrying echoes where shadows stray.

Nature shifts in whispered tones,
Revealing truths that linger, alone.
Every moment, a chance to grow,
In the stillness, the heart will know.

## A Palette of Gentle Shifts

Soft hues blend in twilight's glow,
Brushstrokes dance, a gentle flow.
Colors shift like time's embrace,
Each moment holds a different face.

Dreams ignite in vibrant shades,
Life's canvas, where hope pervades.
Change arrives with every breath,
Painting our souls beyond mere death.

## Floating in Twilight's Embrace

In twilight's arms, we find our peace,
A quiet moment, a soft release.
Stars awaken, secrets unfurl,
As night whispers to this world.

The horizon blurs, day bids adieu,
Starlit paths shine, guiding us through.
Floating softly, fears left behind,
In the embrace of the quiet mind.

## In the Wake of Stillness

In quiet moments, shadows creep,
The world holds secrets, soft and deep.
Whispers of silence fill the air,
In the stillness, one finds repair.

Time slows down, breaths intertwine,
Nature sings, a gentle line.
Under the sky, stars softly gleam,
In the wake of stillness, we dream.

## Subtle Transformations

Leaves turn gold, a quiet change,
Seasons shift, the world feels strange.
Moments pass, yet gently flow,
In subtle transformations, we grow.

A whispered breeze, a tender sigh,
Life transforms as days go by.
From dusk to dawn, a soft embrace,
In the changes, find your place.

## Murmurs of the Heart

In crowded rooms, a soft refrain,
The heart speaks loud, though words are plain.
Every pulse, a tale to tell,
Murmurs of love, in silence dwell.

Eyes connect, a knowing glance,
In every beat, there lies a chance.
Softly spoken, yet so profound,
In the heart's murmur, we are found.

## Veils of Light

Morning breaks, the shadows fade,
A tapestry of light is laid.
Golden hues, a soft caress,
Veils of light, we must confess.

As sunbeams dance on leaves and trees,
Moments captured in gentle breeze.
In every ray, a promise bright,
Life unfolds in veils of light.

## The Still Point of Turning

In the center, silence lays,
Time stands still, the heart obeys.
Moments suspended, whispers blend,
Here, beginnings meet their end.

Thoughts converge in gentle grace,
Lost in time, a sacred space.
Here we linger, dreams unfold,
Stories woven, yet untold.

Light dances on the edge of night,
Softly fades the day's last light.
In this calm, we find our way,
Turning thoughts to where they play.

Breathe in deep, let worries part,
In this stillness, find your heart.
With every turn, a lesson learned,
In the still point, love is earned.

## Tapestry of Silent Moments

Stitches woven, threads entwined,
Silent moments, hearts aligned.
Each passing glance, a story spun,
In this tapestry, we are one.

Colors shimmer, softly glow,
In quiet threads, emotions flow.
Weaving dreams of sweet repose,
Life's intricate dance, no one knows.

A gentle breeze, a whispered sigh,
In this silence, spirits fly.
Each heartbeat echoes, tranquil sound,
In this fabric, joy is found.

Share the moments, cherish tight,
In the stillness, find the light.
Together we create, we mend,
This tapestry with love to send.

## Whispers of Dusk

As the sun sinks low in grace,
Nighttime kisses day’s warm face.
Shadows stretch across the ground,
In the silence, peace is found.

Stars awaken, one by one,
Whispers dance with evening's hum.
In the twilight, dreams take flight,
Cradled softly in the night.

Moonlight bathes the world in silver,
Every heart begins to quiver.
In this hour, our secrets tell,
In the dusky glow, all is well.

Hold the stillness, breathe it in,
A gentle sigh, where we begin.
In every whisper, love ignites,
Whispers linger through the nights.

## The Calm Between Tides

Waves retreat, a quiet space,
In the calm, we find our place.
Moonlit reflections, soft and slow,
Where the gentle waters flow.

Silent shores, a tender pause,
Nature's rhythm, perfect laws.
In this stillness, hearts align,
With the ocean, pure and fine.

Seagulls dance on evening breeze,
Time stands still with perfect ease.
Each moment stretches, soft as lace,
In the tide's embrace, we trace.

Listen close, hear the call,
In the stillness, we stand tall.
With each wave, a promise made,
In the calm, we are remade.

## Peace in Motion

In every breath, the stillness calls,
Gentle waves where silence falls.
The heart beats soft, a rhythmic flow,
In moments bright, we come to know.

With every step, the calm we find,
Threads of joy, we're all entwined.
Whispers dance in twilit air,
A tapestry of dreams laid bare.

Hold the light in open hands,
As love expands, the spirit stands.
In sacred time, let worries cease,
In quietude, we find our peace.

## Fluid Dreams of Calm

In liquid hues, the night unfolds,
A canvas bright where hope consoles.
The stars like soft and tender sighs,
Guide us through the velvet skies.

Drifting thoughts like gentle streams,
We float within our hidden dreams.
A world of peace just out of sight,
In shadows soft, we find the light.

With every heartbeat, rhythms blend,
Together in this journey, we mend.
Tranquil visions appear with grace,
In fluid dreams, we find our place.

## The Color of Tranquil Shifts

Soft pastels brush the morning sky,
As day awakens with a sigh.
Each hue unfolds, a gentle sway,
The promise of a peaceful day.

Nature whispers in shades so bright,
A tranquil dance of pure delight.
Every leaf, a story spun,
In harmony, we are all one.

As time flows on, and moments pass,
Reflections shimmer like polished glass.
In stillness lies the art of grace,
The color of our sacred space.

## Shadows of a Changing Dawn

As dawn unfolds, the shadows play,
In shifting light, the night gives way.
With tender hues that kiss the ground,
Awakening dreams in silence found.

Beneath the sky, the colors blend,
With every breath, a world we mend.
The whispers of a fading star,
Guide us softly, near and far.

Embrace the light as it unfolds,
In shadows rich, the story holds.
With every morning, hope will rise,
A new dawn breaks, beneath the skies.

## Gentle Currents

Softly flows the river's song,
Carrying tales of where it’s strong.
The whispers dance beneath the light,
In harmony, they take their flight.

Beneath the trees, the shadows play,
Drawing dreams from the day.
Leaves flutter in the warm embrace,
As currents weave, they find their pace.

With every ripple, stories blend,
Nature's arms, they gently send.
To unknown shores, hearts drift afar,
Beneath the glow of evening star.

Hushed echoes of the water’s flow,
Silent secrets, time will show.
In gentle currents, we will find,
The peace that lingers, intertwined.

## The Stillness Between Waves

In twilight’s hue, the sea lies calm,
No hasty winds to stir the balm.
Between each rise, in soft repose,
Nature sings where silence grows.

The horizon meets the sky’s embrace,
A fleeting moment, a tranquil space.
Whispers of foam, a gentle sigh,
As moonlight hangs, and shadows fly.

Footprints fade on the sandy shore,
The tide retreats, yet calls for more.
In stillness found, our hearts align,
Like waves at rest in perfect time.

Here we linger, savoring peace,
In sacred pauses, worries cease.
The stillness breathes, a soothing wave,
A quiet strength, steadfast and brave.

## Whispered Transitions

The dawn unveils with softest light,
Day’s quiet breath, a gentle sight.
Whispers weave through the waking air,
Transitions sing, both bold and rare.

Colors shift as shadows play,
Mornings greet the closing day.
With every hue, a story starts,
Binding nature with our hearts.

The flutter of leaves, a fleeting glance,
A dance of time, a sacred chance.
Whispered dreams in the twilight glow,
A bridge between what we know.

Moments linger, brief yet clear,
In whispered transitions, we feel near.
Each passing second, a treasure bright,
In shadows and light, we find our sight.

## Embracing the Quiet Tide

The ocean breathes, a calm descent,
Where whispered waves in silence blend.
Softly lapping at the shore,
Embracing peace forevermore.

The twilight glows on waters wide,
Resting hearts in the quiet tide.
With every swell, the world feels right,
In gentle rhythms, we unite.

Beneath the stars, the night holds sway,
A tranquil dance of night and day.
Where moonlit paths and dreams reside,
In twilight's arms, we seek to hide.

With open hearts, we learn to trust,
In quiet moments, fair and just.
Embrace the tide that rolls anew,
In stillness found, our spirits flew.

## The Quiet Unraveling

In shadows deep, the silence grows,
A thread pulled tight, then gently flows.
The night unveils what hearts conceal,
In whispers soft, we start to heal.

Memories dance on moonlit streams,
Fading softly, like forgotten dreams.
A tapestry of time unwinds,
Each woven thread, the truth it finds.

Gentle echoes linger near,
A melody that calms the fear.
With every breath, the past takes flight,
Into the depths of quiet night.

As dawn approaches, shadows fade,
With tender light, the truth displayed.
The quiet unraveling, we embrace,
Finding solace in each space.

## Beneath Whispered Skies

Beneath the stars, we lay our dreams,
In silver threads and moonlit beams.
The night sky holds our secrets tight,
As whispers weave through velvet night.

Each breath a wish, each sigh a prayer,
In cosmic dance, we shed our care.
The universe listens, ever near,
Beneath the skies, we have no fear.

With every twinkle, stories shared,
Of love and loss, of hearts laid bare.
In starlit depths, we find our way,
With whispered hopes that softly sway.

As dawn approaches, shadows blend,
The sky awakens, day will mend.
Yet beneath the skies, we still believe,
In whispered dreams that never leave.

## A Lullaby for Tomorrow

Close your eyes, let troubles fade,
In dreams of light, a new path laid.
With gentle sighs, the world will rest,
A lullaby that calms the quest.

Tomorrow calls with tender grace,
As shadows dance, we find our place.
Each note a promise, soft and sweet,
In melodies where hearts can meet.

Hold on to hope, let worries go,
In starlit hush, our spirits flow.
Dreams take flight on gentle wings,
From quiet nights, new laughter springs.

As light breaks forth, a brand new day,
With each sunrise, we find our way.
A lullaby that guides us home,
In dreams of tomorrow, we will roam.

## Unfolding Horizons

As dawn unfolds, the world ignites,
With colors bold, in morning light.
Horizons stretch, inviting eyes,
To seek the dreams that fill the skies.

Every step leads to unknown shores,
Where hope is born, and spirit soars.
In whispered winds, our stories told,
Unfolding paths, both brave and bold.

Time dances softly on the breeze,
A symphony that bends the trees.
With open hearts, we chase the sun,
In every moment, life's begun.

The journey calls, a thrilling ride,
Together we walk, side by side.
Unfolding horizons, vast and wide,
In every heartbeat, we abide.

## Veils of Colorful Change

Veils of hues drape the skies,
Whispers of dawn in disguise.
Crimson leaves dance in the breeze,
Nature's art brings hearts to ease.

Golden rays kiss the earth,
Each moment, a brand new birth.
Time transforms day into night,
In colors that ignite delight.

Petals fall as seasons wane,
Memories wrapped in joy and pain.
Change is the cycle we embrace,
In every shadow, find your place.

Beneath the surface, shifts unfold,
Stories written, untold gold.
In every moment, fresh and bright,
Veils of change bring life to light.

**Sails of Tranquil Winds**

Gentle breezes softly blow,
Across the lake, a silver glow.
Sails unfurl, they catch the air,
Peaceful hearts without a care.

Ripples dance on water's skin,
Nature’s song invites within.
Horizons stretch, untouched, unknown,
In tranquil winds, our spirits grown.

Clouds drift by in leisurely grace,
Time slows down, we find our pace.
Eyes that watch the setting sun,
In the stillness, we become one.

Whispers of waves, a soft applause,
Life's sweet rhythms, no need for cause.
With every breath, we gently glide,
On sails of peace, in love we bide.

## The Lull of Life's Undercurrents

Beneath the surface, currents flow,
Silent whispers, secrets grow.
Life's rhythm pulses through the night,
A lull that cradles dreams in flight.

Echoes of time, soft and slow,
Drawing us where shadows go.
Hidden paths intertwine and weave,
In every heart, a chance to believe.

Moments linger like twilight's glow,
Each heartbeat, a story to show.
We drift along the streams unseen,
In life's embrace, our souls convene.

Awakened by the tides of fate,
The lull of life, a gentle state.
In the depths, we learn to see,
The beauty in life's mystery.

## Evening's Subtle Transformation

Evening weaves a tender thread,
Softly cloaking the day's spread.
Colors melt in twilight's sigh,
Stars awaken in velvet sky.

Shadows stretch and whispers call,
Nature’s hush envelops all.
Moonlight spills like silken grace,
Enchanting every hidden place.

Cicadas sing their evening song,
In dusk's embrace, we all belong.
Crickets chirp their soft refrain,
Underneath, the world feels sane.

Moments linger, sweet and still,
Filling hearts with quiet thrill.
Evening's glow, a soft caress,
In subtle change, we find our rest.

## Soft Corners of the Soul

In twilight's hush, the whispers play,
Gentle shadows, where the heart may sway.
Each corner cradles forgotten dreams,
Embracing softness, like silken seams.

A tender touch upon a weary mind,
In the stillness, solace is defined.
With every sigh, a new tale unfolds,
In the warm embrace, the spirit molds.

Fleeting moments, like stars that gleam,
Awakening fragments of a long-lost dream.
Here lies the peace that quietly grows,
In the soft corners, where true love flows.

As dawn breaks through the gentle night,
We find ourselves in softened light.
The soul remembers, we learn to trust,
In every corner, there's love, there's us.

## Waves of Quietude

Upon the shore, the whispers roll,
Waves of quietude serenely unfold.
Each crest a portent of fleeting grace,
Embracing the calm in this tranquil space.

Salt-kissed breezes brush against the skin,
The hush of nature coaxing peace within.
Every ripple, a soft lullaby,
Stirring the heart, teaching how to fly.

Footprints washed away with time's embrace,
Moments linger in the ocean's trace.
A sanctuary where the spirit can roam,
In waves of quietude, we find our home.

The horizon beckons, a distant call,
A promise of solace, where dreams enthrall.
In the rhythm of tides, we choose to sway,
Guided by waves, we'll find our way.

## The Elegance of a Soft Release

In twilight's glow, we learn to let go,
Surrendering burdens, like leaves in flow.
The elegance whispers in gentle sighs,
As freedom dances beneath the skies.

A soft release, where worries fade,
In the space of silence, magic is made.
With each deep breath, the spirit ascends,
Unraveling dreams where love never ends.

Soft whispers mingle with the evening air,
In the act of yielding, we shed despair.
The heart knows the way to heal and restore,
In the elegance found, we become more.

As the stars emerge, lighting the night,
We embrace the calm, surrendering fright.
In the soft release, we reclaim our song,
In the dance of life, we finally belong.

## Transient Taunt of Serenity

In fleeting moments, serenity calls,
A transient taunt as the stillness falls.
Glimmers of peace in a world of haste,
Reminding us gently, beauty won't waste.

A quiet breath in the chaos of day,
Each heartbeat echoes, guiding the way.
Within the soft pause, we find our ground,
In fleeting tranquility, wisdom is found.

Like silken threads weaving through our soul,
Transient taunts that help us feel whole.
In the tapestry woven, we softly tread,
Carrying whispers of what must be said.

As shadows dance in the fading light,
We seek the haven, the respite from fright.
In the transient moments, where silence reigns,
Serenity lingers, and peace remains.

## The Soft Canvas of the Mind

Thoughts paint colors bright and bold,
Dreams whisper stories yet untold,
In the silence, creation sways,
A canvas waiting for its days.

Brushstrokes of memory, gentle and light,
Each hue a moment, each shade a flight,
Wandering freely, the heart finds rest,
In the vast expanse, it feels so blessed.

Imagined landscapes, vast and wide,
Where ideas flourish and fears subside,
Upon this canvas, life takes shape,
Endless wonders, the mind's escape.

So let the colors blend and merge,
In the soft canvas, let passion surge,
Crafting worlds with every thought,
In this realm, the soul is caught.

## The Quiet Dance of Shadows

Beneath the moon's soft, silver glow,
The shadows stretch and ebb like flow,
In whispered secrets, they entwine,
A dance of silence, so divine.

They sway on walls, a fleeting trace,
In corners dark, they find their space,
With elegance, they'll softly glide,
In the stillness, they abide.

Hidden stories in their forms,
A mystery wrapped in norms,
With every movement, they appear,
A ephemeral waltz, so clear.

In the night's embrace, they softly play,
Time dissolves in shadows' sway,
An artful ballet, unconfined,
In the quiet dance of the mind.

## Serenity Between the Melodies

In the spaces where silence lays,
A gentle calm, a soft malaise,
Between the notes, a peace aligns,
Where heart and rhythm intertwines.

The whispers dance in soft refrain,
Like raindrops falling on a windowpane,
Each pause a breath, each gap a gift,
In music's ebb, our spirits lift.

Echoes linger, a subtle art,
Between each phrase, there lies the heart,
In tranquil moments, we find our way,
As melodies guide our care away.

So let the music softly rise,
In serene spaces, let joy surprise,
For in this hush, our souls can fly,
Creating peace where sweet notes lie.

## The Glow of Softening Light

As daylight fades, shadows extend,
The glow of dusk, it seems to blend,
With hues of amber, rose, and gold,
A tender sight, a story told.

The world transforms in twilight's grace,
Each corner brightens, finds its place,
The heart ignites with gentle fire,
In evening's hold, we find desire.

Softening light upon the ground,
In its embrace, peace can be found,
Every ray, a whispered kiss,
In the transition, there's pure bliss.

So linger here, in the fading day,
Let the glow guide you on your way,
For in the twilight's tender sweep,
Our dreams awaken, our souls can leap.

## Radiance of Slumbering Thoughts

In quiet corners, whispers dwell,
Beneath the surface, dreams compel.
A gentle glow in twilight's gaze,
Illuminating misty ways.

Each thought a spark, a glimmer bright,
Through darkened paths, they seek the light.
A tapestry of wishes spun,
In slumber's embrace, we are one.

Hidden depths of silent schemes,
Awakening softly from our dreams.
A breath away from realms unknown,
The heart within begins to moan.

So let us cherish this deep night,
Where slumbering thoughts take silent flight.
For in their radiance, we find
The secret truths of heart and mind.

## Essence of Peaceful Moments

A quiet breeze through swaying trees,
Whispers of calm, a sweet release.
The world slows down, a gentle sigh,
Where time itself learns how to fly.

Soft sunlight filters through the leaves,
As nature sings and softly breathes.
In every heartbeat, silence sings,
The essence of peace that stillness brings.

With every step upon the earth,
We find the beauty of our worth.
In tranquil waters, reflections gleam,
Moments of peace, like a serene dream.

Let us embrace these fleeting hours,
In every raindrop, in blooming flowers.
For peace resides in hearts that care,
Essence of moments, forever rare.

## Serenity in the Sculptor's Hands

From marble stone, a vision wakes,
In sculptor's hands, creation takes.
Each careful stroke, a dream is found,
As silence breathes, and shapes abound.

With every chisel, a whisper flows,
Revealing grace where beauty grows.
A dance of light on polished skin,
Serenity dwells deep within.

The patience held, the soft embrace,
Unveils the hidden form and face.
In focused stillness, beauty blends,
The sculptor's art, where spirit transcends.

Through timeless hands, the stone recalls,
A legacy as spirit calls.
In every curve, in every line,
Serenity's mark, forever divine.

**The Grace of Changing Seasons**

When autumn leaves begin to fall,
A tapestry of golds enthrall.
The crispness in the morning air,
Announces change with gentle flair.

As winter blankets earth in white,
The world transforms, a stunning sight.
In stillness, beauty finds its form,
In icy wonders, calm and warm.

As spring unfolds with tender blooms,
A symphony of sweet perfumes.
With every petal, life awakes,
A dance of color as it shakes.

And summer beams with warming rays,
Where laughter spills in sunlit days.
The grace of seasons flows anew,
In every heart, a vibrant hue.

## Transitions in Twilight

The sun dips low, a gentle sigh,
Colors merge in a soft goodbye.
Shadows stretch, as whispers creep,
Night unfolds, inviting sleep.

Stars awaken, one by one,
A canvas dark, where dreams are spun.
The breeze carries secrets untold,
In twilight's glow, life unfolds.

Mists rise slowly from the ground,
In silence, a new path is found.
Leaves rustle, a soft embrace,
Time shifts in twilight's grace.

With every change, a promise grows,
In the dusk, where magic flows.
Embrace the night, let worries fade,
For in transitions, dreams are made.

## Ebb and Flow of Silence

The ocean whispers, soft and low,
Tides retreat, then gently flow.
Every wave a lullaby,
In silence deep, we learn to fly.

Footprints left in sand so fine,
The fleeting moments intertwine.
As echoes fade into the night,
We find our peace, our inner light.

Between the breaths, a heartbeat rests,
In quietude, our spirit nests.
The world may roar, but here we stand,
In silence, together, hand in hand.

Ebb and flow, like whispered dreams,
Life's gentle dance, or so it seems.
With every pause, we grow and know,
In stillness lies our deepest glow.

## The Dance of Stillness

In the quiet, shadows play,
A gentle waltz, both night and day.
Leaves sway softly with the breeze,
Nature's dance brings hearts to ease.

Moments frozen, time holds breath,
In stillness, we confront our depth.
A fleeting glance, a knowing smile,
In silence, we bridge every mile.

Thoughts like clouds drift high above,
In stillness blooms the fragrant love.
As time unwinds in soft retreat,
The rhythm pulses, slow and sweet.

The dance of stillness, pure and true,
Guides our hearts to renew,
With every step, we learn to see,
In quietude, we're truly free.

## Veils of Soft Transition

Mornings break with a golden hue,
The world awakens, kissed anew.
Veils of mist in the early light,
Dance like dreams, taking flight.

Colors shift as the hours go,
Life evolves, a steady flow.
Every heartbeat, every sigh,
Marks the moments passing by.

As day turns to dusk's embrace,
Time casts shadows, a gentle trace.
In the twilight, we find our place,
Veils of change, a soft embrace.

With every ending comes a start,
In transitions, we find our art.
Through the veils, new worlds are spun,
In soft transitions, we are one.

## Soothing Echoes

Soft whispers dance in the night,
Gentle breezes take their flight.
Stars awaken, one by one,
Painting dreams until the dawn.

The silence sings a tender song,
Where the heart feels it belongs.
Moonlight bathes the world in grace,
Tranquility in every space.

In the shadows, secrets dwell,
Stories only silence tells.
Every echo finds its way,
Guiding souls where hearts can sway.

Close your eyes and breathe it in,
Let the soothing echoes begin.
In this moment, peace aligns,
Woven gently, heart redefines.

## The Calm Before the Canvas

Blank pages hold a world of dream,
Colors await the artist's theme.
Brush in hand, the heart beats fast,
In stillness, inspiration cast.

Every hue a whisper soft,
In the silence, visions loft.
A palette rich with hopes untold,
Promise of a story bold.

Feel the tension, crisp and clear,
Moments echo, drawing near.
Each stroke dances, wild and free,
Capturing the soul's decree.

Before the chaos, calm prevails,
In the silence, spirit sails.
Unveiling worlds both bright and vast,
In the quiet, visions last.

## Destinations of Quietude

Paths unwound in the still of night,
Finding solace in twilight's light.
Whispers linger upon the breeze,
Nature's voice, a gentle tease.

Mountains stand with wisdom vast,
Guardians of time, unsurpassed.
Rivers flow with stories deep,
In their arms, we fall asleep.

Fields of green embrace the soul,
Here, the heart can feel its whole.
Every step a soft reprieve,
In this peace, we learn to believe.

Destination reached, we sigh,
Underneath the endless sky.
In quietude, we find our way,
Unraveling life, day by day.

## Swaying in Still Waters

Gently rocking on the tide,
In stillness, we confide.
Reflections whisper in the night,
Cradled softly, holding tight.

Ripples dance with grace and ease,
Carrying tales on the breeze.
Moonlit paths invite to roam,
Swaying softly, finding home.

Among the reeds, secrets swirl,
Nature's magic begins to unfurl.
A tranquil heart knows how to flow,
In stillness, we find our glow.

Beneath the surface, dreams reside,
In still waters, time's our guide.
Swaying gently with the night,
Embracing peace, pure delight.

## Ebbing Dreams

In twilight's glow, dreams softly fade,
Whispers of hopes in shadows laid.
Forgotten wishes drift like leaves,
Carried by winds that no one believes.

Memories linger, as the night calls,
Beneath the stars, where silence sprawls.
A gentle tide pulls thoughts away,
Ebbing quietly into the gray.

Once vibrant colors, now worn and pale,
Echoes of laughter, a distant tale.
Waves crash softly on shores of time,
Rhythms that pulse with a weary rhyme.

Yet in the depths, a faint spark glows,
A promise of dreams, no one knows.
Though shadows grow, and darkness schemes,
Hope shall arise from ebbing dreams.

## The Calm Before Change

A silent hush, a breath held tight,
The world awaits, cloaked in night.
Stars blink softly, as if to say,
Tomorrow will bring a brand new day.

In the stillness, a heartbeat throbs,
Nature pauses, as time absorbs.
Clouds gather whispers, a storm in mind,
A dance of fate, beautifully blind.

Promises linger just out of reach,
Lessons of love that time will teach.
With every dawn, a choice unfolds,
The stories of old, in new hands, retold.

But here, in the calm, all is serene,
A fleeting moment, caught in between.
For change will come like the tide's embrace,
Renewing all with its boundless grace.

## Chasing Solitude

In wooded depths, where silence reigns,
I tread softly on nature's lanes.
Whispers of trees call my name,
In their embrace, I find no shame.

The brook sings songs of tranquil peace,
As gentle ripples invite release.
Away from clamor, away from the race,
In solitude's arms, I find my place.

Golden leaves dance in the breeze,
A quiet moment that never flees.
Time stands still as I listen close,
Chasing solitude, I find what I chose.

With every heartbeat, I grow more whole,
Nature's symphony fills my soul.
In the stillness, I shed my fear,
Embracing the silence, I hold it dear.

## Fragments of Peace

A broken glass on the table lies,
Reflecting light in fractured skies.
Yet in each shard, a story breathes,
Fragments of peace the heart retrieves.

In quiet corners where shadows creep,
Gentle murmurs begin to seep.
Soft whispers of solace weave anew,
Between the chaos, hope breaks through.

Petals drift down from withered blooms,
In colors soft, dispelling glooms.
Every tear, an ocean deep,
Carries the weight, yet lifts to keep.

In every loss, a lesson remains,
In every struggle, the heart gains.
Embracing the fragments held so tight,
We find our peace, in the darkest night.

## The Poetry of a Liquid Heart

In tides that swell, emotions flow,
A heart like water, soft and slow.
It whispers secrets, drips of dreams,
Through bends of love, pure moonlit beams.

With every wave, a story sighs,
Reflecting truths beneath the skies.
A liquid dance, both wild and free,
Embracing every new decree.

Each drop a memory, cherished, dear,
In every flood, a fleeting tear.
Yet calm it stays, a silent stream,
Where passion flows, yet stays a dream.

So let it pulse, this tender art,
The endless poetry of the heart.
In ripples soft, we find our way,
In liquid love, forever stay.

## Serene Transitions

The dawn arrives, a gentle glow,
With hues of pink, a soft hello.
The night retreats, a dream once spun,
As daylight breaks, the journey's begun.

In whispers calm, the breezes shift,
Through golden fields, a quiet gift.
With every hour, a new embrace,
In colors lost, we find our place.

As shadows fade, the world transforms,
Through tranquil paths, the spirit warms.
Each step we take, a heartbeat's song,
In moments shared, we all belong.

So let us dance through time's expanse,
In serene transitions, take a chance.
With open hearts, the journey flows,
In every change, the beauty grows.

## Subtle Changes in the Air

A whisper stirs, a fleeting sigh,
Beneath the clouds, the dreams will fly.
As seasons shift, the essence sways,
In twilight's grace, the heart obeys.

The leaves will rustle, softly speak,
In hidden trails, a path unique.
Each breath we take, a tale unfolds,
In gentle winds, our truth beholds.

Through morning's fog, a quiet rise,
In subtle hues that touch the skies.
Awakening worlds, a dance of light,
Where quiet changes spark delight.

So let us pause, and feel the shift,
In subtle changes, life's sweet gift.
For in the breeze, we find our fate,
In every breath, we contemplate.

## The Silence of Places Unknown

In valleys deep, where shadows lay,
The silence speaks in shades of gray.
Each stone recalls, a time long past,
In stillness held, the echoes cast.

Among the trees, where whispers hide,
Secrets linger, a patient guide.
In every nook, the stories weave,
A tapestry of what we believe.

The air is thick with dreams unshared,
In hidden realms, hearts laid bare.
Embracing night, the stars extend,
The silence wraps, a gentle friend.

So wander forth, into the dim,
In places unknown, let hopes begin.
For in the still, the heart will see,
The silence speaks, eternally.

## The Embrace of Gentle Currents

In the hush of twilight's glow,
Whispers weave through waters slow.
Softly cradling dreams untold,
Currents dance, a tale unfolds.

Beneath the stars that shimmer bright,
Sailing shadows fade from sight.
With each wave, a secret shared,
In its depths, a heart laid bare.

Endless ripples, tender flow,
Carrying hopes where breezes blow.
Nature's sigh, a sweet embrace,
Wandering souls find their place.

## Ethereal Touch of Quiet Change

In the garden where shadows fall,
Time slips by, a gentle call.
Petals sway in whispered tune,
Evening melt into the moon.

Colors blend as daylight fades,
Nature sighs in soft cascades.
Each moment shifts like painted skies,
Unseen threads where silence lies.

Fragile breath of twilight grace,
Threads of silver interlace.
Change arrives, though soft and slow,
In its hush, we come to know.

## The Weight of Gentle Moments

In a pause that holds the air,
Time stands still, a silent prayer.
Each heartbeat marks a fleeting scene,
Treasures found, yet unforeseen.

Hands entwined, a soft embrace,
Every glance a sacred space.
In the stillness, worlds unfold,
Woven tales, both bright and bold.

Yet the moments drift like sand,
Captured fleeting, slip from hand.
But in memory, we retain,
The gentle weight of soft refrain.

## Hues of Silent Reflection

In the stillness, colors blend,
Shadows whisper, currents send.
Crimson dreams in twilight gleam,
Thoughts awaken, lost in dream.

Each hue tells a secret story,
Fragments bathed in gentle glory.
Reflections ripple through the night,
Guiding souls to find their light.

Yet in silence, answers flow,
Silent lakes and softest glow.
In the depths, an inner peace,
Find your heart, let worries cease.

## Cascading Moments of Clarity

In whispers soft, the dawn awakes,
A gentle breeze, the silence breaks.
Each thought cascades like flowing stream,
Illuminating every dream.

Beneath the haze, a spark ignites,
In fleeting time, we find our sights.
With every moment, truth unfurls,
Revealing layers of our worlds.

The echoes dance in shadows bright,
Guiding hearts toward the light.
In clarity, we learn to see,
The hidden paths that set us free.

So breathe in deep, let worries go,
Embrace the now, and let it flow.
For in this space, we're never lost,
In moments clear, we count the cost.

## Rippling Reflections

In stillness lies a mirrored pond,
Where thoughts like ripples drift beyond.
Each reflection shines a new fate,
A dance of dreams we contemplate.

The water weaves a tale so deep,
Of secrets held in silence keep.
With every wave, the past entwined,
A clearer view of what we find.

When shadows stretch and light cascades,
The heartbeats synchronize, parade.
Each drop contains a universe,
In rippling depths, we're not diverse.

So cast your gaze upon the glass,
Each moment fleeting, none shall pass.
In reflections bright, we learn to swim,
In water's flow, our spirits brim.

## Tranquility Unbound

Underneath the quiet sky,
The world asleep, a soothing sigh.
In stillness held, the heart can soar,
To realms where chaos is no more.

Each breath a wave, soft and wide,
In tranquil seas, we find our guide.
The whispering winds, a gentle call,
In moments hushed, we rise, we fall.

The stars above, they twinkle clear,
In solitude, we hold them near.
In peaceful fields where thoughts align,
Serenity is not confined.

So let the stillness fill your soul,
In nature’s arms, we find our role.
With open hearts, we break the mold,
In tranquility, our stories told.

## The Art of Letting Go

In every breath, a chance to free,
The weight we carry, let it be.
Each moment clings, yet must depart,
The gentle art of open heart.

Through rising tides, we learn to swim,
With each stride taken, no need to dim.
To release the pain, embrace the joy,
In every tear, a precious ploy.

With autumn leaves, they fall so grace,
A reminder time will leave its trace.
What once was held can find new ground,
In letting go, our peace is found.

So cherish what the past can teach,
But unearth the dreams that lie in reach.
For in surrender, life will flow,
The art unfolds in letting go.

## A Journey Through Still Waters

Upon the glass where silence sleeps,
Reflections dance in gentle sweeps.
A lonely boat on tranquil seas,
Embraces whispers of the breeze.

The sun dips low, the shadows blend,
Each ripple tells where dreams transcend.
In pause, the heart finds space to soar,
To taste the peace it longs for more.

Beneath the sky, a canvas wide,
In stillness, worries slip aside.
The journey calls, the spirit free,
As water flows, so shall we be.

With every stroke, the water glows,
A soothing balm where time slows.
In still waters, we find our way,
A journey lived in soft array.

## The Poetry of Unseen Currents

In hidden depths where shadows play,
A current stirs, both night and day.
Beneath the calm, a rhythm flows,
The poetry that nature knows.

Each wave a word, each splash a rhyme,
In silent verse, they speak of time.
With every pulse, the waters speak,
In whispered tones, their secrets leak.

An unseen dance beneath the hue,
A tapestry of life anew.
Through silent whispers, tales unfold,
Of journeys sung and stories told.

To feel the depths, we must let go,
Embrace the current's gentle flow.
For in the unseen, truths arise,
And through the depths, the spirit flies.

## Windows to Whispered Calm

Through panes of glass, the world shines bright,
A tranquil scene, a heart's delight.
Each framed view holds a moment still,
In whispered calm, the soul can fill.

The trees are swaying, softly sway,
While sunlight dances, shadows play.
In every glance, a peace we find,
As nature speaks, we intertwine.

The azure sky, a canvas wide,
Invites us in, where dreams abide.
Through windows, we observe the grace,
Of fleeting time, a sacred space.

Embrace the peace, let life unspool,
In whispered calm, we are the fuel.
Through windowed hearts, we seek and yearn,
For whispered truths that gently burn.

## Silk Threads of Transition

In twilight's glow, the fabric shifts,
With silk threads woven into gifts.
The past releases, the future waits,
In transitions soft, a journey grates.

Each thread a moment, fragile, fine,
A tapestry where we define.
As colors blend, the stories change,
In every stitch, life feels arranged.

The autumn leaves, a gentle fall,
Each spiral dance, a herald's call.
To let go means to embrace,
The spiraling dance of time and space.

With every seam, we shape our fate,
In silk threads spun, we contemplate.
For transitions lead to new sunrise,
A woven path where dreams arise.

**Layers of Timeless Stillness**

In the quiet shade of trees,
Whispers ride upon the breeze.
Time stands still, or so it seems,
As we wander through our dreams.

Echoes fade in gentle light,
Moments linger, pure delight.
Hidden truths beneath the sound,
Stillness wraps the world around.

Softly falls the evening glow,
Stars emerge, a gentle show.
In this peace, our spirits blend,
Timeless love that knows no end.

Through the night, the silence sings,
Wrapped in warmth, the heart takes wing.
In the layers, we find grace,
In stillness lies our sacred space.

## The Silence Within Waves

Beneath the roar of ocean tides,
A quiet place where calm abides.
The whispering foam, a soft embrace,
In waves, we find our secret space.

Rippling thoughts like water flow,
In gentle currents, time moves slow.
The silence held within each crash,
Brings fleeting moments, soothing splash.

Lost amidst the endless blue,
Connections deep, the heart anew.
In every swell, a story wakes,
The silence within each wave stakes.

With the moon's pull, the sea aligns,
In tranquil depths, stillness shines.
In every tide, a lesson learned,
From silence, wisdom is discerned.

## The Flicker of Peaceful Thoughts

Amidst the chaos of the day,
Flickers come, then fade away.
Peaceful thoughts like candles glow,
Guiding hearts through ebb and flow.

In still moments, we can breathe,
As gentle whispers weave and wreathe.
A tranquil mind, a tender grace,
Finds warmth in quiet, safe embrace.

With each flicker, fears dissolve,
Through peaceful thoughts, our hearts evolve.
Seeking solace in the night,
We dance with dreams, bathed in light.

Hold each flicker close and dear,
Let it guide you, calm your fear.
In the dawn, as shadows play,
Peaceful thoughts will lead the way.

## Whispers of the Unfurling Day

Morning light begins to rise,
Birds take flight across the skies.
Whispers soft, the world awakes,
In dawn's embrace, a silence makes.

Blooms unfold with gentle grace,
Nature breathes in slow embrace.
Every leaf, a story tells,
Each petal caught in morning's spells.

Colors brush the canvas wide,
In this beauty, hearts abide.
With every moment, love's array,
Whispers echo, fade away.

As the sun climbs high above,
Filled with hope, and tender love.
In the hush of the breaking day,
We find ourselves, come what may.

## The Dance of Shadows

In the dusk, they sway and weave,
Silent whispers, tales they leave.
Footsteps traced in twilight's grace,
Memories lost in time and space.

A flicker here, a shiver there,
Figures glide without a care.
Shapes that linger, fade away,
Caught in twilight's muted play.

Chaos twirls, yet peace is found,
Softly echoing all around.
In the stillness, secrets blend,
As shadows dance, the night extends.

With every turn, they form and break,
An endless waltz, a gentle ache.
In their rhythm, life aligns,
In the dance, eternity shines.

## Liquid Tranquility

A calm river beneath the sky,
Gentle ripples quietly sigh.
Reflections of a world so bright,
Whispers dance in the soft light.

Serenity flows with each breath,
In liquid depths, we conquer death.
Time slows down, a sacred space,
Where worries fade without a trace.

Pebbles rest on the riverbed,
Stories of all that they have shed.
Beneath the waves, the secrets bind,
In tranquil waters, peace we find.

The essence of life in each swirl,
Embracing the calm, the world unfurls.
In liquid arms, fears drift away,
In still reflection, hearts will stay.

## Harmonies of Flux

Notes entwine in a playful breeze,
Melodies dance among the trees.
Every rustle, a song begins,
In the chaos, harmony spins.

Colors blend in vibrant strokes,
Life's tapestry, it softly provokes.
Change is constant, yet it's divine,
In every moment, stars align.

Rhythms pulse through nature's heart,
Life’s composition, every part.
In the tempo, joy unfolds,
Through shifting tales that time beholds.

Echoes of laughter, whispers of pain,
In the flux, we rise again.
Finding balance in every sway,
Harmonies guide us on our way.

## Echoes of Softness

A tender hush in the starlit night,
Embracing dreams, a soothing light.
In whispers soft, the heartbeats blend,
With every sigh, we gently mend.

Velvet shadows wrap around,
A cocoon of love, safe and sound.
Moments linger, sweetly shared,
In this softness, we are bared.

Fingers trace on silken skin,
Every touch ignites within.
In tranquil pause, our spirits soar,
As echoes of softness beckon more.

Time suspends in the quiet air,
A bond of souls beyond compare.
In every whisper, we find our place,
In echoes of softness, we embrace.

## Breath of the Wandering Mind

In shadows deep where thoughts reside,
Whispers call from the other side.
A flicker here, a spark anew,
The wandering mind, forever true.

Amid the silent drift of night,
Curious dreams take graceful flight.
A tapestry of hopes unfurled,
In this vast, enchanted world.

Each breath a tale, a fleeting chance,
Where fleeting moments twist and dance.
The heartbeats echo, softly chime,
In the breath of the wandering mind.

Lost in realms where fantasies roam,
Every thought a chance to roam.
With open skies and endless seas,
The mind's embrace, a gentle breeze.

## Embers of Soft Reflection

In twilight's glow, the embers gleam,
Inviting echoes of a dream.
Reflections dance on water's face,
Soft whispers of a warm embrace.

With every flicker, stories told,
Of moments cherished, memories bold.
The heart ignites with gentle fire,
In the embers, we find desire.

As shadows stretch and daylight fades,
The world transforms in soft cascades.
Beneath the stars, we find our way,
To the warmth of night from day.

Let thoughts alight like moths in flight,
As embers sparkle in the night.
In every glimmer, a life shines bright,
Soft reflections in the moonlight.

## Tides of Gentle Embrace

Waves caress the sandy shore,
In whispers soft, they yearn for more.
Like tender arms around the land,
The tides draw close, a lover's hand.

With each ebb, a secret kept,
In salty breeze, the ocean wept.
A dance of water, wild and free,
In tides that sing serenity.

The moon commands, a silver reign,
While stars hold tight the night’s sweet gain.
Together, they weave a song so true,
In cycles old, forever new.

Each rise and fall, a heartbeat’s grace,
In tranquil moments, find your place.
Let the waves wash away your fears,
In the gentle embrace of years.

## Moments Where Stillness Hides

In quiet corners of the mind,
Amidst the chaos, peace we find.
A fleeting breath, a silent sigh,
In moments where stillness hides.

Between the tick of time’s own clock,
In softest spaces, hearts may dock.
A pause to breathe, a chance to see,
The beauty in simplicity.

The world may whirl, the noise may rise,
But here stillness claims the skies.
In gentle folds of time's embrace,
Moments bloom, a sacred space.

So seek the stillness when it calls,
In hidden nooks, behind the walls.
For in each silence, life abides,
In cherished moments where stillness hides.